As illustrated here, Trump is said to like his suits, shirts and ties all to be in solid colors. Donald is the only candidate with his own clothing label, the Donald J. Trump Signature Collection. The line includes shirts, suits, ties, leather accessories and eyewear.

PLATE 2

Donald Trump graduated with a bachelor's degree in economics from the Wharton School of Business in 1968.

PLATE 1

Married to Melania Knauss since 2005, perhaps wife #3 is Donald's lucky charm. He was married to first wife Ivana Zelníčková from 1977 to 1992, and to second wife Marla Maples from 1993 to 1999. Interestingly, Trump claims to be good friends with both exes.

PLATE 3

Trump was once a big
investor in the hotel/
casino business that
included Trump Taj
Mahal built on the
famous Boardwalk
in Atlantic City, NJ at
a cost of nearly one
billion dollars. But his
ventures in the glitzy
world of gaming and
hospitality went into
bankruptcy several
times and are no longer
under his ownership.

PLATE 4

Donald Trump bought Miss Universe, Inc., which also includes the Miss USA and Miss Teen USA pageants, from the business owner of the beauty pageant in 1996. In the wake of controversial comments Trump made on the campaign trail, he recently sold his interests to the American talent agency/sports marketing giant WME/IMG.

PLATE 5

"You're fired!" was the catchphrase for the popular *Apprentice* and *Celebrity Apprentice* reality television shows that Donald Trump hosted from 2004–2015. Contestants on the original version of the show vie for a chance to win a contract to run a Trump business, while those on the celebrity spinoff compete to win money for a chosen charity. Recently NBC ended its relationship with the billionaire businessman and signed Arnold Schwarzenegger to host the upcoming season of the program.

PLATE 6

GENUINE BONA FIDE
Trump University
DIPLOMA

Donald displays a "diploma" from his now-defunct online educational site, Trump University. The unaccredited educational business was not a university in any legal sense, and the school, which promised to share secrets to real estate success, stopped operating.

PLATE 7

Trump was a part of the immensely popular "Battle of the Billionaires" at WrestleMania 23 in 2007. The event was a hair vs. hair feud pitting Trump's pro-wrestling representative against WWF chairman Vince McMahon's rep. The loser agreed to shave his head. Trump got to keep his golden locks and clearly enjoyed shaving McMahon's head in front of the roaring crowd. In 2013, Trump was inducted into the WWE's Hall of Fame.

PLATE 8

Donald Trump poses as a human "tie rack," displaying samples of one of the many merchandise lines offered in the Trump "brand"—conservatively designed neckties in primary colors and traditional patterns.

PLATE 9

Donald Trump loves to play golf and even wrote a book about it called *The Best Golf Advice I Ever Received.* He owns well over a dozen golf properties and has spent millions refurbishing courses that include U.S. locations in New York, New Jersey, Florida, North Carolina, Virginia, and California, as well as courses in Scotland, Ireland and Dubai.

PLATE 10

Trump doesn't own a pilot's license, but he does own a customized Boeing 757 jet airliner. The plane seats up to 43 VIPs buckled in with 24-carat gold-plated seatbelts. It has a master bedroom with silk-covered walls, a queen-size bed, and customized entertainment system plus a master bath complete with a shower and gold-plated fixtures. There is also a wood-paneled galley, dining room, guest bedroom, and a main lounge with a 57-inch screen and a state-of-the-art entertainment system with 1,000 movies and 2,500 CDs on tap.

PLATE 11

Trump has promised to build a wall along the 2,000-mile U.S.–Mexican border and make Mexico pay for it. Many fact-checking organizations estimate that the project would cost between $10 billion to $12 billion, and that getting the Mexican government to fund the endeavor is simply wishful thinking on the part of the candidate.

PLATE 12

Some politicians have referred to Trump as a carnival barker. But "The Donald," a natural-born showman and the ultimate self-promoter, currently leads in the Republican presidential contest despite their labeling.

PLATE 13

Trump's hard line anti-immigration message encouraged his supporters and enraged his critics. It has sparked both applause and outrage among people of all ages, races, and religions and it's no doubt that the debate over American values and ideology will continue well beyond the race for president.

PLATE 14

Between 1987 and 2014, Donald Trump has written or co-written eighteen nonfiction books, from *Trump: The Art of the Deal* to his most recent, *Crippled America: How to Make America Great Again.* "The Donald" has plenty to teach his eight grandchildren!

PLATE 15

Donald Trump as superhero—prepared to do battle with his opponents to win the 2016 Presidential election.

PLATE 16